Quick & easy

Cat & Kitten Care

Kelli A. Wilkins

Quick & Easy Cat & Kitten Care

Project Team
Editor: Brian M. Scott
Copy Editor: Carl Schutt
Design: Patricia Escabi
Series Design: Mary Ann Kahn

T.F.H. Publications
President/CEO: Glen S. Axelrod
Executive Vice President: Mark E. Johnson
Publisher: Christopher T. Reggio
Production Manager: Kathy Bontz

T.F.H. Publications, Inc.
One TFH Plaza
Third and Union Avenues
Neptune City, NJ 07753

Library of Congress Cataloging-in-Publication Data
Wilkins, Kelli A.
Quick and easy cat and kitten care / Kelli A. Wilkins.
p. cm.
Includes index.
ISBN 0-7938-1034-5 (alk. paper)
1. Kittens. 2. Cats. I. Title.
SF447.W66 2005
636.8–dc22
2005013133

This book has been published with the intent to provide accurate and authoritative information in regard to the subject matter within. While every precaution has been taken in preparation of this book, the author and publisher expressly disclaim responsibility for any errors, omissions, or adverse effects arising from the use or application of the information contained herein. The techniques and suggestions are used at the reader's discretion and are not to be considered a substitute for veterinary care. If you suspect a medical problem, consult your veterinarian.

The Leader In Responsible Animal Care for over 50 years!™
www.tfhpublications.com

Printed and bound in China

06 07 08 09 3 5 7 9 8 6 4 2

Table
of Contents

Choosing a Cat or Kitten

Introducing a kitten or cat into your life is a big decision. Before you bring a pet into your home, take some time to carefully consider all the responsibilities you'll be adopting. Owning a pet is a lifelong commitment that should not be taken lightly. No matter what age, gender, or breed of cat your new pet is, he or she will be relying on you to provide for all of his or her needs. The following questions will help you decide if you are ready to take care of a cat or kitten:

- Am I willing and able to provide my cat or kitten with the proper daily care he will need for the rest of his life? (Cats can live 20 years or longer.)

- Will I accept the financial cost of owning and caring for a kitten or cat? (Expenses such as food, supplies, and veterinarian visits can add up to hundreds of dollars per year.)

- Will I take my cat to the veterinarian if he becomes ill?

- Do I have enough space in my home for an indoor cat or kitten?

- Is anyone in my family allergic to cats?

- Are there other pets already living in the house?

- Do I have young children or infants in the house?

- Will I set aside the necessary time it takes to groom my cat?

- Will I scoop out the litter box, feed the cat, and supply him with fresh water each day?

- Is there someone I trust who can take care of my cat or kitten if I go away on vacation?

If you've considered all the requirements and are excited about getting a kitten or cat, then you're on your way to responsible pet ownership. Now you have several other choices to make before you bring home your furry friend.

Kittens are full of energy and love to explore new things.

A Kitten or Two

If you decide to adopt a kitten, why not get two? The kittens can keep each other company and play together when you're not home. They will also learn how to socialize and interact with another animal. A single kitten will need a constant playmate and may feel lonely and isolated after he's been taken away from his mother and littermates.

Kitten or Cat?

If you had a choice between adopting a cuddly kitten or an adult cat, which would you choose? Do you have a preference at all? Some pet owners are set on owning a kitten so they can watch him grow up, while other people prefer a full-grown cat. Every cat owner is different, just as every cat (or kitten) is different. Both kittens and adult cats make great pets—so how do you choose between them?

Kittens

Kittens are ready to leave their mothers at about 12 weeks of age. By this time, they have been weaned off their mother's milk and should be eating solid food. Kittens are just starting out in the world, and everything is new to them. This means that your kitten will be relying on you to teach him everything he needs to know about living with people (and perhaps other pets or adult cats).

Depending on where you get your kitten, he or she may need to be neutered or spayed. This is a one-time expense, but it can be costly. Kittens will also need a variety of immunizations during their first year, and this will require multiple visits to the veterinarian.

When you bring a kitten into your home, you will have to train him how to behave and teach him what not to do (such as scratch the sofa or climb the drapes). Kittens are full of energy and are high spirited, so be prepared. They love to explore their surroundings and will want to play at all hours. A kitten will demand a lot of your attention, and you will need to act as his "mother" and help him adjust to living with you. Keep in mind, however, that your cuddly kitten will grow up to become an adult cat—it's inevitable.

Cats

Adult cats are generally more settled and serene than kittens. An adult may already be spayed or neutered and will mostly likely be vaccinated. Adult cats know how to behave and have a good concept of the "rules" of living with people. They are less likely to dig up a potted plant or splash around in their water bowl for fun.

If you adopt an adult cat, take into consideration that the cat has a history that may be unknown to you. The cat will have already established habits and preferences for certain types of food, cat litter, and life in general. Depending on where you obtain the cat, you may be able to learn something about his background, such as his name, if he was an only cat or lived in a multiple-cat household, if the previous owners had children, or if his personality is laid back, friendly, or shy.

Adult cats are generally less active compared to kittens.

Quick & Easy Cat & Kitten Care

Adopt an Adult

Many adult cats are put up for adoption because their owners move, have children, or the cat is no longer an adorable little kitten. By taking an adult cat into your home, you give an unwanted pet a second chance to have a good life.

An adult cat will not be as high spirited as a kitten and will not want to race around the house chasing toys at all hours of the night. Adult cats sleep more than kittens do and generally average 12 to 18 hours of sleep per day (and require more sleep as they grow older).

Purebred or Moggy?

A purebred cat or kitten is no more loving or devoted than a random bred (or mixed breed) known as a moggy. A purebred is descended from one particular breed of cat and has a long breeding history. Show-quality cats are purebred cats that are raised and bred by breeders. A show-quality cat must meet the specific "breed standards" with regard to size, hair length, and coloring.

Purebreds and show-quality cats and kittens can cost hundreds of dollars (if not more), so if you're not planning on showing or breeding your cat (or kitten), a moggy is probably just right for you. However, if you absolutely love a particular breed of cat and want to own a purebred, check out your local animal shelter or rescue organization. Many breeders often put purebreds up for adoption because they aren't show-quality and do not meet one of the breed standards. This has no effect on the cat's or kitten's ability to make a wonderful pet. (The cat doesn't know if he's a purebred or not.) Unwanted moggies and purebreds have a lot of love to give to their owners and are waiting to find a happy home.

Some pet owners prefer males over females and others the complete opposite. In the end, the decision is all yours.

Male or Female?

Whether you choose a male or female cat or kitten is entirely up to you. Some cat owners prefer one gender over another, and to some, it doesn't matter at all. In general, it makes no difference because kittens and cats of both sexes are great pets.

Male cats are generally larger and heavier than females. A "complete" or unneutered male will spray urine to mark his territory. Neutering (or castrating) the male before puberty will stop this behavior. It is less expensive to neuter a male, and the procedure can be done as soon as the veterinarian recommends it. This is usually around 6 months of age.

Female cats tend to be a little smaller than males. They generally reach sexual maturity between 6 and 12 months of age and will look for a mate when they are in estrus (also known as "being in heat"). Female cats should be spayed when they are between 6 and 8 months old to prevent them from reproducing. Spaying is a more complex procedure involving removal of the cat's reproductive organs, and it costs more than neutering.

Some people believe that spayed females turn cold and unfriendly and that neutered males act more loving toward their owners, but there is no scientific proof that this is true. All cats and kittens have their own personalities, and no matter what gender you adopt, your kitty will be like no other.

If you have adopted an adult cat, he or she may already be spayed or neutered. Some pet adoption agencies make it a policy to spay or neuter all cats and kittens before they go to their new homes.

Long-Haired or Short-Haired Coat?

The length of a cat's coat (or hair) may influence your choice in adopting a particular pet. Hair length is a matter of personal choice. Some cat owners enjoy the daily brushing and combing necessary to keep a long-haired cat's coat tangle free, while others are content to give their short-haired cat a weekly or monthly brushing.

New cat owners should know that the long-haired breeds (such as Persians, Ragdolls, and Maine Coons) will require daily grooming. Their long fur can become tangled, matted, and clumped if it is not taken care of. Long-haired cats are also more susceptible to hairballs than short-haired breeds because they swallow a great deal of hair while grooming themselves.

Long-haired breeds need daily brushings so their coats stay healthy and untangled.

Short-haired breeds (such as the Egyptian Mau, Burmese, and Siamese) have shorter hair and require less grooming. These cats need occasional brushing and combing—once a week to once a month, depending on the cat's coat. If you do not want to spend time each day vacuuming your home and brushing a long-haired cat, consider adopting a short-haired breed.

Finding Your Feline

Whether you want to adopt a kitten or a cat, there are several places where you can find a feline, such as animal shelters and rescue organizations, pet adoption web sites, ads in local newspapers, and pet stores.

Animal Shelters and Local Rescue Organizations

The best place to find a kitten or cat awaiting adoption is at your local animal shelter or humane society. Each day, people bring in unwanted cats and kittens and place them up for adoption because they no longer want the responsibility of keeping them. Animal

Many animal shelters are loaded with cute kittens, like these two that are in need of a good home.

rescue organizations are another great source for finding a cat or kitten. Many local rescue organizations are small, independently run, not-for-profit shelters that rely on volunteers to stay in business.

When adopting a cat or kitten from a shelter, ask the following questions:

- Does the pet come with a health guarantee?

- Has a veterinarian examined the cat or kitten? (If so, get the vet's name, address, and phone number.)

- What does the adoption fee include?

- Has the cat or kitten been spayed or neutered?

- How old is the animal? (Most places will be able to give you an approximate age.)

- What background information (if any) is known about the cat or kitten? (This can include the reason the cat or kitten was dropped off, his or her name, what the family life was like, if the cat or kitten has had his or her shots, what type of food the kitten or cat was eating, etc.)

There will be an adoption process you will have to undergo (such as filling out an application, supplying references, answering questions about your experience in pet ownership, and in some cases, a background check). Don't let this process discourage you from finding a loving pet. The adoption agency wants to make sure any animal that leaves their facility is going to be cared for properly and will live in a loving environment.

Pet Adoption Web Sites

Pet adoption web sites (such as Petfinder.org) list cats and kittens available for adoption from shelters, rescue organizations, and private homes. These web sites can help you locate cats and kittens in your local area that are in need of a second chance.

Choosing a Cat or Kitten 13

Sometimes you can even find purebreds among the animals that are up for adoption.

After you've contacted the local organization about the cat or kitten you're interested in, you can pay them a visit and meet the animal in person. The adoption agency will determine if you are a good match for the cat. Then, if all goes well, you can take your newfound friend home. Pet adoption web sites are an easy way to find a pet (they also have dogs, reptiles, birds, and small mammals available for adoption), and everyone benefits in the long run.

Newspaper Ad

Many times you will see "Kittens—Free to Good Home" ads in the newspaper. In most cases, the cat's owner has an unexpected litter of kittens on his or her hands and just wants to get rid of them. If you decide to adopt one of these kittens, ask a lot of questions and try to obtain as much information as you can about the kittens, the mother cat, and the owner. Find out:

- the age of the kitten(s)
- if the kitten is weaned
- what the kitten has been eating
- what (if any) vaccinations the kitten has had

- if the kitten has been examined by a veterinarian
- if there is a health guarantee with the kitten
- if the owner will take the kitten back if a vet doesn't give the kitten a clean bill of health
- the overall health and vaccination record of the mother cat
- why the kitten is being given away
- if the owner has any other cats or pets in the house

Be sure to get the owner's name, address, and phone number so you can follow up if you have any questions or concerns later. If the owner seems uneasy or does not want to answer your questions, be suspicious of his or her motives, and keep looking for a pet. You don't want to unwittingly adopt an ill kitten.

Pet Stores

All too often, the cats offered for sale at pet stores are obtained from "backyard breeders" or kitten mills. (These irresponsible breeders add to the pet overpopulation problem by breeding animals for profit.) At these pet stores, you may not be able to find out any information about the cat's or kitten's history or background (such as where he originally came from and what kind of conditions he was living in).

However, not all pet stores are like this. There are good ones that sell cats and kittens from quality breeders. One of these good stores will be able to tell you the name of the breeder, give you a history of the kitten you are buying, offer a complete health guarantee, and provide a vaccination and medical record. The kittens will be kept in a clean and spacious area with toys and will be well socialized. Additionally, the store staff should be friendly and knowledgeable about the cats, and the other animals they sell.

Ask Questions

No matter where you obtain your cat or kitten, be sure the place where you are adopting your pet from passes inspection. When you go to the animal shelter, rescue organization, or private home, ask yourself the following questions:

- Is the establishment clean or are there any unpleasant odors (like cat urine)?
- Is the place overcrowded?
- Is the staff (or owner) helpful and willing to answer your questions about the cat or kitten?
- Are the cat's or kitten's living conditions up to par (clean food and water bowls, a tidy litter box)?

Take a good look around and ask a lot of questions. Be wary of anyone who tries to hurry you into making a quick decision or someone who will not let you look around or handle the cats. Trust your instincts and leave if something doesn't feel right.

Choosing a Healthy Cat

Now that you've thought about what kind of cat or kitten you want (if you have a preference) and you know where to find a feline, you need to recognize the signs of a healthy cat or kitten. In addition to checking out the cat's living conditions, take some time to examine the cat or kitten up close. Here are a few things to look for:

Pet Adoption Days

Large pet supply stores frequently host pet adoption days. The stores provide space to local animal shelters and rescue organizations, so they can find homes for unwanted pets. The stores do not actually sell the animals, but rather act as a "middleman" and allow people looking for kittens and cats to view the animals available and meet with shelter representatives. This is a good alternative way to find a cat or kitten in your local area.

You're Adopted

Sometimes you don't have to go looking for a cat or kitten—sometimes one finds you. If you find yourself adopted by a stray cat, you won't have a choice with regard to gender or age. Before you take a stray into your home and adopt him or her as your own, you should run a "Found Cat" ad in the local newspaper. The cat or kitten may have gotten lost and someone may be anxiously looking for him. Give a good description of the cat or kitten including gender, eye color, and markings. While you're waiting for a response to the ad, make the stray warm and comfortable, but keep him away from any other pets you have. The animal may be ill, and you don't want to make your own pets sick.

If a few weeks go by and the cat's original owner hasn't claimed him, take the cat or kitten to the veterinarian for a complete checkup. Explain to the vet that you found the cat as a stray and have no medical history or background on the animal. The vet will give the cat a complete checkup and the necessary vaccinations.

- Check the coat and skin. Run your hands down the cat's body. The cat's coat should feel smooth and look shiny. (A kitten's fur may feel fuzzy or fluffier than an adult cat's.) There should be no patches of missing fur, scabs, sores, or lumps on or under the cat's coat.

- Watch the cat walk. Make sure he isn't limping or behaving awkwardly. (A cat that walks "off balance" may have a medical problem.)

- Check the cat or kitten for fleas. Part the fur in a few random places and look for fleas or flea droppings. If you find tiny specs that look like black pepper, the cat or kitten has fleas.

- Check the eyes, ears, nose, and teeth. The cat's or kitten's eyes should be clear and free of residue in the corners. The ears should not look dirty, have waxy buildup, or smell foul. The nose should feel warm and dry, not runny or crusty. The cat's gums should be pink and there should be no missing teeth.

- Feel the cat or kitten. Does he or she seem to be a good weight for his or her age and size? You shouldn't be able to see or feel ribs sticking out of the cat's sides, but the cat shouldn't look obese, either.

- Pick up the cat or kitten. Handle the cat for a few minutes. How does he react to being touched? Does he squirm and resist, or accept your touch? Does he purr and want to be petted?

- Try to bond with the cat or kitten. Sit on the floor and call the cat to you. If he comes, play with him, pet him, and see how he reacts to being around you. This should give you an idea of the cat's personality.

Be cautious of choosing any cat or kitten that doesn't seem interested in anything happening in his or her surroundings. Cats and kittens do sleep a lot, so if you wake one up from a nap, he will be groggy, but he should be curious as to what is going on. If the cat hasn't been napping recently and seems very confused or lethargic, he could be ill.

No matter what kind of kitten or cat you adopt, make sure you are ready to give him a good home and take care of him for the rest of his life. The choice is yours—male, female, moggy, purebred, long-hair or short—they all make great, loving pets.

Housing Your Cat or Kitten

Now that you've decided on a new feline companion, you need to get everything ready for the day you bring your cat or kitten home. With a little preparation, you can make your pet's transition into your home a safe and stress-free experience.

Getting Ready

Your new pet will need some "moving in" supplies. It's a good idea to buy everything you'll need ahead of time. Take a trip to your local pet supply store and purchase the following items:

- a pet carrier
- food and water bowls
- cat (or kitten) food
- a litter box and a scoop
- cat litter
- cat toys
- a scratching post
- a cat bed
- brush and comb
- a collar and ID tag
- leash or harness (optional)

Your kitten or cat will need these supplies when he or she comes to live with you. Once you know what to look for, shopping for these items will be easy.

Pet Carrier

Your new cat or kitten will need an appropriately sized pet carrier. Purchase a carrier that will be large enough for your pet when he or

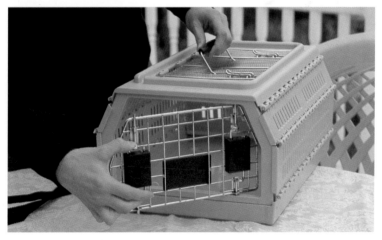

Always have a sturdy pet carrier available to transport your cat or kitten in.

When traveling with your cat or kitten, never leave your pet unattended in the car—even if you leave the windows cracked open. The temperature inside the vehicle can reach deadly temperatures in minutes.

she is full grown, even if you're adopting a kitten. If you are adopting two kittens (or two cats) get two carriers. Each cat should always have his or her own cat carrier.

The carrier should be made of sturdy plastic and must have a securely locking door. Be sure the carrier has good ventilation and is designed so that it is easy to take the kitten (or cat) in and out of. The cat will want to look around and see where he is going, so look for a carrier with an open-faced grill type door. The carrier should also have a solid, secure handle and a sturdy base. Place an old towel on the bottom of the carrier to give your cat or kitten a soft place to rest while traveling.

Cheap cardboard boxes are not recommended for use as cat carriers. Their bases and handles are very flimsy, and a determined cat or kitten can easily claw his or her way out. Cardboard carriers are often dark, trap heat, and do not allow adequate ventilation for pets.

Food and Water Bowls

Earthenware or ceramic food and water bowls are best for your pets. These types of bowls are sturdy and easy to clean. Plastic bowls can become scratched and harbor harmful bacteria that can make your cat or kitten sick. A curious kitten may decide to play with a lightweight plastic bowl and flip it over or move it around the floor for fun. If you are adopting a kitten, make sure you purchase "kitten sized" food and water dishes. These bowls are smaller and shallower than a bowl designed for a full-grown cat. A tiny kitten could be intimidated by a huge bowl of water and he may not be able to reach down into the bottom of a larger bowl to eat.

If you have more than one cat or kitten in your home, provide each pet with a set of his or her own food and water dishes.

Cat or Kitten Food

Pet food manufacturers make many different types of cat and kitten food (including dry food, semi-moist, and canned) in a variety of flavors. A kitten will need to be given food specially designed for growing kittens, but an adult cat should only be given food designed for adult cats.

If you know the type and brand of cat or kitten food your pet was eating before you brought him home, buy the same type and feed it to your pet. Switching brands or types of food can make a new arrival confused or stressed.

Litter Box and Scoop

There are many types, sizes, and styles of litter boxes on the market today. You can purchase a self-cleaning litter box, one with a hood, or a plain plastic litter box. The style of litter box you buy is a matter of choice—yours and the cats.

Self-cleaning boxes have a mechanism that rakes the dirty litter after your cat has used the box. Although these boxes make your cleaning job easier, they are more expensive than other types of boxes. The

Quick & Easy Cat & Kitten Care

automated process that cleans the box can frighten a cat (and especially a kitten) who has never used this type of litter box before.

A hooded litter box is a plastic box with a tall cover that snaps onto the rim. This type of litter box is designed to give the cat some privacy, while shielding the actual box from view. One advantage to this type of litter box is that the cat cannot toss litter over the edge of the box and make a mess. However, some cats are intimidated by the hood and do not like the "enclosed" feeling they get while using the box. The hooded litter box is very dark on the inside and it can trap odors if the hood does not have adequate ventilation.

In some cases, the litter box will come with a plastic scoop. The scoop should have slits in the bottom to allow you to sift the litter in the box and scoop out the waste.

If you have a kitten, purchase a "kitten-sized" litter box. These boxes are smaller than a regular litter box and have low sides that allow the kitten to climb in and out of easily. It's recommended that you start your kitten out using a regular plastic litter box because an automated or hooded box could frighten the small kitten.

A plastic litter box is inexpensive and can be purchased at most grocery stores. These boxes are open to the air and allow the cat to climb in and out easily.

If you have adopted an adult cat and you know what type of litter box he or she was previously using, buy the same kind. If you try to change the style, the cat may become confused or refuse to use the litter box.

Cat Litter

There are many types of cat litter available for cat owners today, including clay, silica crystals, and clumping litter. The type you use is your choice, but if you know what kind of litter your cat or kitten was using before, continue using it.

Non-clumping clay litter is the most common type of cat litter. This inexpensive litter is made of absorbent clay and is available in several varieties, such as dust-free, dust-reduced, scented, and unscented types.

Cat litter crystals are made from silica gel and are designed to evaporate moisture. This is a very absorbent, dust-free litter that is great for preventing cat odors. Cat litter pearls are made from silica sand and absorb liquid without clumping.

Clumping cat litter is designed to form semi-solid clumps of litter when wet. This type of litter makes cleaning the box easier because all the liquid waste has been turned into clumps. However, clumping cat litter is not recommended for use in homes that have

Pick a Good Place

When setting up your pet's "bathroom" accommodations, choose a quiet spot in your home. Place the litter box in a place that's easy for the cat to get to and is in an area of your home that doesn't get a lot of activity. Most people set up the cat's litter box in a spare bathroom or bedroom.

Quick & Easy Cat & Kitten Care

Always keep your kitten's litter box fresh and clean.

kittens. If the kitten walks through a wet patch of litter and then licks his feet, he could ingest the clumping material. This could lead to a serious blockage of the intestinal tract.

Cat Toys

Cat toys are a must for any cat owner. All kittens and cats love to play—and they'll play with just about anything they find. There are a vast number of cat and kitten toys available on the market today, so you're guaranteed to find toys your cat or kitten will enjoy playing with. Cats and kittens like to chase and pounce on things, so you may want to start out with simple, fun toys such as balls and catnip-filled mice.

Whatever type of toys you choose for your cat or kitten, you must make sure that they are safe for your pet. Be sure they do not contain anything that can be chewed off or fall off and become a choking hazard. Play it safe and avoid:

- toys with small parts like tiny bells or glued-on plastic eyes (a cat can choke on them)
- toys with feathers (they can be broken off and swallowed)

A Bag Is Not a Toy

Keep plastic bags away from your kitten or cat. Although your pet may want to play in the bag, it is not a toy. If the bag handles slip over the cat's head they could wrap around his throat, and the cat could suffocate.

- small foam balls (the cat can chew off the foam and swallow it)
- marbles, bells, or anything small enough to go down the cat's throat

Examine all toys before you buy them or you let your kitten or cat play with them. If a toy is becoming worn or gets cracked, replace it with a new one. Keep a good supply of toys on hand for your cat or kitten. (This is especially true if you have more than one cat in the house.) They will like a variety of playthings to choose from.

Scratching Post

All cats and kittens scratch as part of their natural behavior. In the wild, cats scratch on trees and other objects to mark their territory (they have a scent gland on the bottom of their footpads), to shed the sheaths of their claws, and to stretch. Therefore, your cat or kitten is going to need at least one scratching post. If you have more than one cat, you'll need to give each cat his or her own scratching post.

There are many kinds of scratching posts available to cat owners, and most are made of wood covered with thick carpet. You can find kitty condos that double as scratching posts and hideaways, as well as multi-level cat towers that allow the cats to perch up high and view their surroundings.

The post you buy should be tall enough so your cat can stand up on his back legs and get in a good scratch and stretch. Be sure the post has a secure and wide base so the cat cannot tip it over and get hurt.

This is especially true if you have a tiny kitten at home.

Cat Bed

Cats love to sleep, and they tend to make their bed anywhere that looks comfy. Some cats prefer to find their own cat bed, which can be in your closet, on your bed, or even in a cardboard box. Even though your cat may have his or her own ideas about sleeping arrangements, you should provide your cat or kitten with a bed of his own.

There are many types of scratching posts available to cat owners. Pick one that best fits both your cat and your home décor.

There are many types of cat beds available, and they are often lined with flannel or cotton to give the cat a comfortable place to nap. The cat bed should be large enough for the cat or kitten to curl up in, but not too big. Cats like to feel secure where they sleep and touching the sides of their bed gives them a sense of security.

Place the cat bed in a quiet area of your home where the cat is not likely to be disturbed. In time, the cat or kitten will move right in.

Brush and Comb

All cats need some assistance with their grooming, so you'll need to purchase a brush and comb designed especially for cats. The type of brush and comb set you buy will differ depending on the type of cat you have. For example, if you have a long-haired Persian, you will have to buy a brush and comb made for grooming long-haired cats. Smaller, softer brushes and combs are available for grooming kittens. You can find a variety of grooming supplies available at your local pet store.

Collar and ID Tag

Every pet should wear a collar with an ID tag at all times. If your cat or kitten should leave the house (or escape through an open door) and get lost, the collar and tag will let the person that finds him know where the cat belongs.

The collar should have an automatic release that will disengage if the cat gets caught up on something (like a tree branch). When buying a collar, get one that fits your cat properly. Collars come in a variety of sizes based on the size and weight of your pet. If you have a kitten, he or she should be given a "kitten sized" collar. As the kitten grows, you will need to buy him or her a larger collar.

When attaching the collar, leave enough space for two fingers between the cat's neck and the collar. You want the collar loose enough so the cat can breathe and swallow easily, but not so loose that the cat can slip out of the collar. Your cat or kitten might not like the feel of the collar around his neck at first, and may squirm and struggle to pull it off. This is normal. After a few days, the cat will adjust to the collar and forget that he is wearing it.

The identification tag should have your name and phone number on it, along with the pet's name. Some pet supply stores have automated machines that make engraved ID tags for you in just a few minutes. You can also order tags from pet supply catalogs or from pet supply web sites online.

Leash and Harness

If you decide to take your cat or kitten for an outdoor walk, you'll have to buy a leash and/or harness for your pet. Leashes and harness are available at pet stores and come in a variety of sizes and styles. Be sure to buy the proper size for your cat or kitten. The harness should fit snugly, but it shouldn't be too tight that you cannot slip two fingers between the harness and the cat's body. Give your kitten or cat time to

Microchips

Cat owners are now able to have their lost pets returned to them by using high-end technology instead of relying on a metal ID tag. You can have your veterinarian inject an identifying computer chip into your cat or kitten. The microchip is injected under the muscle near the shoulder and cannot be lost or removed by the cat. This doesn't harm the cat, and the chip can be inserted in a kitten at about eight weeks of age.

If your cat is found and turned into an animal rescue organization or shelter, workers will scan the cat for a microchip and use the special code to find the cat's owner. This relatively inexpensive procedure is a good way to ensure that your lost pet will be returned to you. If you have your cat microchipped, be sure to update your contact information if you move.

Some collars are more extreme than others.

adjust to wearing the harness or leash inside the house before you venture outside.

Keeping Your Cat Safe

It's important to safeguard your home before your new kitten or cat arrives. Adult cats that have been living with people will probably ignore most of the things they know are off limits to them. Kittens, however, get into everything and will need to learn what to avoid.

There are many household dangers in the average home, most of which you probably aren't even aware of. If you've never owned a cat before, get down on your hands and knees and take a look around from your cat's (or kitten's) point of view. You'll be amazed at how many hidden dangers you'll find.

In general, keep your kitten or cat away from anything that he or she can swallow and choke on. This includes everyday objects such

Chairs with soft, fluffy cushions are an immediate attraction to cats.

as: buttons, bones (that may be picked from the garbage), coins, dental floss, jewelry, medication, nails, paper clips, pen tops, rubber bands, screws, and staples. These items may make fun "found" toys, but they are choking hazards. Keep small objects off the floor and out of reach.

Heat sources such as fireplaces, woodburning stoves, kitchen stoves, and ovens are also dangerous to your cat. A kitten may want to investigate what you've just taken out of the oven or may be attracted to the heat given off by a wood stove. If a curious cat jumps onto a hot stove or gets too close to the fireplace, he could get burned. Teach your cat or kitten that these heat sources are off limits.

Candles are another common household danger to cats. The flickering light from a candle fascinates most cats and kittens and they naturally want to investigate. Never leave a lit candle unattended—not even for a few minutes. If your cat or kitten decides to "play" with the flame, he could get seriously burned and start a fire.

Appliances can also be hazardous to your pets. Before you bring a kitten or cat home, make sure that the kitty cannot squeeze under, behind, or into any appliances (including refrigerators, stoves, and dishwashers). Keep the doors closed on your washer and dryer, and make sure the toilet lid is down. (A tiny kitten could fall in and drown, or the lid could close on him and cause an injury.)

Kittens especially like to explore, and they will find hazards that you never even knew existed.

Holiday Hazards

Although the holidays are fun times for most people, they can be dangerous for your cat or kitten. Seasonal decorations such as Christmas trees, glass ornaments, metal hooks, tinsel, garland, ribbons, bows, and festive candles are all potential dangers to your cat. Many kittens are drawn to shiny objects and want to play with ornaments dangling off a Christmas tree. They could shatter a glass ornament, get a hook caught in their paw, or even knock the tree over. Don't let your kitten or cat climb the Christmas tree or drink water from a Christmas tree stand.

Electrical cords are another source of potential danger. Keep your pets away from extension cords and electrical outlets. Kittens may chew on the cords or play with them. Keep the cords out of reach or buy cord holders designed for use in homes with small children.

Keep all chemicals such as drain cleaner, bleach, toilet bowl cleaners, pool sanitizers, etc. away from your cat or kitten. These items are extremely toxic and can be lethal if ingested. Remember that your cat or kitten walks on the floor, so be sure to rinse the floors well after they've been washed. If the cat gets residue from cleaning products on his paws and licks them, it could make him sick. If you have your house exter-minated or use bug bombs, take your cat to a friend's or neighbor's home until your house is aired out. Cats have delicate systems, and the chemicals used could be toxic to your pet.

Be sure that appliances are always checked before closing any doors or drawers, as they can be hazardous to you pets.

Recliners and Kittens

If you have a small kitten in the house, always check the furniture—sofas, recliners, and swivel chairs—before you sit down. Sometimes a kitten will crawl into or under a piece of furniture to play or take a nap. If the kitten gets trapped, the results could be deadly. Be sure to teach all the members of your family about "cat-proofing" your house and overall cat safety.

Although they may be nice to look at, some plants are poisonous to cats and kittens. It's a good idea to know what kind of plants you have in your home and to know if they are toxic. If you do have poisonous plants, keep them away from your cat or kitten. You can place the plants in a room that is off limits to the cat, hang the plants from hooks, or place them on high shelves. Some common poisonous plants include:

aloe vera	marigold
azalea	mistletoe
baby's breath	morning glory
daffodil	peony
Easter lily	philodendron
eucalyptus	poinsettia
geranium	primrose
holly	tiger lily
iris	tulip

A full list of poisonous plants can be found at www.aspca.org.

Indoors Only

One of the best ways you can ensure the safety of your cat or kitten is to keep him or her indoors at all times. Although some pet owners argue that keeping a kitten or cat "cooped up" for his entire life is like a cruel prison sentence, it's actually humane. An "indoors-only" cat or kitten will not have to face the dangers and perils of the outside world such as poisonous antifreeze or insect repellent, traffic, heatstroke, frostbite, dangerous altercations with other animals (such as dogs, raccoons, or territorial cats), and nasty people who don't like cats. Cats that are allowed to wander outside can also pick up parasites (such as fleas and ticks) and contract diseases from other cats. Remind family members to always close doors and windows so the cat or kitten does not accidentally get outside.

If you want to give your cat a safe outdoors experience, you can purchase a secure pen or cage for your cat. These pens (or runs) will allow your cat to sit outside and get fresh air, yet he will not be able to wander off and get into trouble. If you do buy a cage or pen for your pet, make sure the cat cannot escape and that other animals cannot break into the cage. If you don't have room in your yard for a cat-run, keep your pet indoors—you just may save his life.

Antifreeze

Antifreeze is deadly for cats and other animals. Keep your cat out of the garage and store antifreeze where your pets cannot get to it. You may want to purchase environmentally friendly, nontoxic antifreeze instead of the traditional kind.

When Your Cat Comes Home

Once you have cat-proofed the house, it's time for kitty to come home. Remember, everything is new for a cat or kitten when he or she comes into your house. An adult cat has lived in a house with people before and generally knows what to expect, but a young kitten may be overwhelmed by the sudden change. Don't just bring the kitten home, open the cat carrier, and let the kitten run free— he will be scared and won't adjust to his new home properly.

Before you bring your cat or kitten home, set up a room for the new arrival to call his own for a while. The room should be in a part of the house (such as a spare bedroom or bathroom—not the basement or garage) where the cat can hear and smell people.

Put everything the cat or kitten will need in this room, (food and water dishes, litter box, cat bed, scratching post, toys) let the cat out of the cat carrier, and show him where the litter box is. (If you have a small kitten, you can place the kitten in the litter box and make some scratching motions with his paw. The kitten will understand what you're trying to tell him.)

Let the cat or kitten explore his room on his own. He'll probably be a little on-edge and may hide, or he might start exploring and sniffing everything. Give him time to adjust. A young kitten may be skittish and scared at first, so try not to make any sudden moves. (Don't lunge at the kitten and try to pick him up.) Above all else, be patient. Talk to the cat in a soothing voice and give him something to eat. Play with the cat or kitten for a while so he begins to bond with you.

After a day or so, you can slowly start introducing other family members to the kitten or cat. Let the cat smell everyone and get to know his new family at his own pace. Try to keep the crowds down. Although everyone will be eager to see the new pet, too many people in the room at once will overwhelm or stress your cat. If you do not have other pets in the house, you can let the kitten or cat out of his room to explore the rest of your house when you feel that he or she is ready.

Cats and Kittens Living With Other Cats
If you have other cats in the house and you bring home a new cat, you'll have to let them get to know each other—slowly.

One way to introduce two cats (or a kitten to a cat) is to let the established cat sniff the new arrival under the door to the temporary room. This will allow them to get to know each other, and prevent any fighting. Remember that an adult cat is much larger than a

A new cat will probably be a little on-edge when he first arrives. Let him have some time to adjust.

small kitten, and your kitten may be afraid of the "big" cat. Cats are territorial and the established cat may hiss or growl at the scent of a newcomer in "his" house. Kittens usually won't be jealous or territorial toward another kitten—instead they may just start playing together.

Another option is to place the new kitten in his cat carrier and let the two cats see and sniff each other through the carrier. After a while, you can switch the cats and place the established cat in her or her own carrier and allow the new cat to wander and sniff the established cat. When you feel that the two cats are ready to meet face to face, introduce them to each other. Spend time petting, grooming, or playing with each cat in turn, so one does not get jealous of the other.

Remember

Before you bring your new cat or kitten home, make sure that he has received a checkup and all his necessary vaccinations. This is especially important if you have other cats in the house.

Watch how the cats interact and be prepared for some degree of growling, hissing, or swiping at each other. This is natural at first. When the cats become familiar with each other and establish a hierarchy, everything should settle down. Don't leave the cats alone until you're sure they won't fight. If a fight does break out between the two (or you suspect one is brewing) separate the cats and reintroduce them the next day.

Cats and Kittens Living With Children

If you have children in the house, they must be taught that the kitten or cat is a live animal with feelings and should be treated with respect. Make sure you teach your children how to behave around a kitten or cat (whether the pet is yours or belongs to someone else). They should not pull the cat's ears or tail, yell at the cat, scare the cat, or tease it for fun. Show them how to pet the cat gently.

If you think your children are old enough to make friends with the new cat (or kitten), show your child how to pick up and hold a cat properly. The best way to hold a kitten or cat is to:

1. Approach the cat slowly and quietly so you do not startle him.

2. Pick up the cat under the chest (near the shoulders).

3 Hold the cat (or kitten) close to your chest .

4. Support the cat's legs with your hand or arm so his legs don't hang free in midair. (This will give your pet a feeling of stability and comfort.)

If the cat squirms or struggles, put him down gently.

Young children should be taught to be especially careful around kittens—a tiny kitten could inadvertently get stepped on. Never let a small child walk around carrying a kitten or cat. The child could squeeze, drop, or accidentally hurt your pet in another way.

Always let the established cat sniff the new arrival before they are permanently housed together.

The age a child is allowed to bond with a cat depends on the child's maturity level and the personality of the cat. Use your judgment and evaluate the situation based on what you know about the child and the cat. Preschoolers and young children should always be supervised when playing with, petting, or picking up a cat or kitten. As the child matures and understands how to interact with the cat, he or she can be left alone with the cat. Remember, don't leave small children alone with a cat or kitten—you never know what might happen.

Feeding Your Cat or Kitten

Making sure your pet gets the proper nutrition is vital. Kittens and adult cats have different feeding requirements, so it's important that you feed your pet a balanced and healthy diet.

Feeding Kittens

A growing, active kitten requires more calories than adult and senior cats. Kittens need more fats, proteins, vitamins, and taurine (an essential amino acid) in their diet compared to adult cats. The best way to ensure your kitten is receiving the proper nutrients is to feed him or her food specially designed for kittens. The "kitten formula" food should be clearly

Weaning

Kittens are usually weaned from their mothers at around six to eight weeks. If you've adopted an orphaned or stray kitten that hasn't been weaned, you can feed the kitten a milk supplement until he is old enough to eat solid food. Your veterinarian can provide you with the proper food supplement and give you detailed instructions on how to feed the kitten.

marked that it is nutritionally complete and balanced for growing kittens.

There are many quality name brands of kitten food available in your grocery store and in pet supply stores. Pet food manufacturers make kitten food in a number of flavors in dry, semi-moist, and canned varieties. Kittens should be fed kitten food for their first year, because this is when they do most of their growing.

Feeding Adult Cats

Adult cats don't need the high-calorie food that kittens do. In fact, feeding an adult cat kitten food will make him or her fat, fast. In addition to the "regular" types of cat food on the market, there are

All cats should be offered a food that is nutritionally complete and properly balanced.

Feeding Seniors

many specialty formula foods available for adult cats. Pet food manufacturers have created specialty foods for dental care, hairball control, special "senior" food, food for overweight cats, food for cats with urinary tract problems, and even food designed for indoor cats. Contact your vet if you think your cat should have a "specialty" food for a specific nutritional need. He or she can advise you on the correct type of food for your adult or senior cat.

Quality Counts

You may feel a bit overwhelmed when it comes to buying cat or kitten food. There are a lot of brands, types, formulas, and flavors on the market today. The most important factor to keep in mind when choosing food for your cat or kitten is that the food is a good-quality brand and has all the necessary nutrients your pet needs.

Avoid buying "no name" or generic brands of cat and/or kitten food. These products are usually low-grade food and often do not

Taurine

All cats and kittens must have a diet that includes taurine. This amino acid is essential for their health. A cat or kitten that has a taurine-deficient diet could develop eye problems, and in some severe cases, blindness. Make sure that taurine is listed as an ingredient in whatever food you feed your cat or kitten.

Not Hungry?

If your cat or kitten stops eating, he may be upset about something. Have you changed brands or flavors of cat food, or brought another pet into the house? If so, the cat could be on a "hunger strike" as a form of protesting the change. If you haven't changed anything around your home and you cannot get the cat to eat, take him to the vet for a checkup. Loss of appetite is a sign of illness, and your cat could be sick.

have the essential vitamins and minerals your cat (or kitten) needs.

Brand names and premium cat foods contain all the necessary ingredients your cat needs to stay in good health. Brand names are usually less expensive than premium brands and are available in your local grocery store or pet supply store. Premium brands are more expensive and can be purchased from most veterinarians.

Well-known name brands or premium brands of cat food are the best choices for your pet.

No matter what brand of food you buy, always take a few moments to read what is listed on the box (or bag, or can). A bag of cat (or kitten) food labeled with the words "meets the nutritional levels for a complete diet" or "provides complete and balanced nutrition as established by the Association of American Feed Control Officials (AAFCO)" is a good brand. Read the ingredients. A good quality cat or kitten food should contain a minimum of 4 percent taurine and should not be filled with sugar, food dyes, or preservatives.

Food Dishes

Each cat or kitten should have his or her own set of food and water dishes. Separate bowls will prevent fighting over food and ensure that each kitty gets enough to eat. If you have a multiple-cat household and need to feed kitten food, regular adult food, and a senior blend, separate dishes will ensure that each cat gets the right type (and portion) of food.

Feeding Your Feline

Your cat or kitten will let you know when he is hungry. There are two feeding options available to cat owners, self-feeding or scheduled feeding. You can allow the cat or kitten to "self-feed" by leaving dry or semi-moist food out all day for him. The cat will be able to eat or snack whenever he wants. This is a good option for people who are at work all day.

If you feed your cat canned food, you'll have to set up a regular feeding schedule so the canned food does not spoil. Set up a specific time (or two) during the day to feed your cat. (The schedule you set can be based on your schedule, such as before you go to work, or when you come home for the day.) Keep in mind, however, that once you set this schedule, you have to stick to it. The cat or kitten

Changing Food

Cats are creatures of habit and don't like change, especially when it comes to their food. If you have to switch brands (or flavors) of food, do it slowly. Mix some of the new food in with the old kind and increase the percentage of new food into the mix each day. This gradual change (over seven to ten days) will allow your cat to adjust to the new food. If you suddenly switch brands or flavors, your cat could become finicky and refuse to eat the new food.

will be relying on a regular feeding time, and he will let you know when dinner is late. If you use scheduled feedings for a kitten, make sure you offer him food two or three times a day. Kittens burn more calories than adult cats and need more frequent feedings.

How Much to Feed

Read the bag, box, or can of food before you feed it to your kitten or cat. Pet food manufacturers list their recommended feeding portions somewhere on the packaging. Follow the pet food manufacturer's portion guidelines to determine how much to feed your cat.

Make sure that your cat or kitten has a good supply of fresh, clean drinking water available at all times.

Water

Water is essential. Your cat or kitten must have access to fresh, clean water at all times. This means that you must wash out the water dish and replace the water every day. Some cats are messy eaters and may drop food bits into the water bowl. If this happens, change the water at once. Your cat won't want to drink water that has something floating in it.

If your cat or kitten doesn't seem to be drinking much water, don't worry. Believe it or not, cat and kittens obtain most of their required moisture through the food they eat. Canned food is about 75 percent water and is a good source of moisture. Semi-moist cat food is approximately 35 percent water. Dry food ranges from 6 percent to 10 percent water, depending on the brand. No matter what type of food you feed your cat or kitten, make sure he or she always has clean water available.

Grooming Your Cat or Kitten

Although cats are clean animals and they bathe themselves daily, your cat or kitten will need some basic grooming assistance from you. Start a regular grooming regimen when you bring home your new cat or kitten. The earlier you start grooming your pet, the more readily he or she will adjust to it. Your cat will eventually come to see grooming as a part of everyday life.

If you adopt an adult cat, be patient when you start grooming him (or her). The cat may never have been groomed before (or was only groomed minimally) and he or she may not like it at first.

Above all else, make the grooming ritual a pleasant time for your pet. Talk to your cat or kitten in a soothing voice and offer him a small treat as a reward after the grooming session is complete. With a little patience and perseverance, your kitten or cat will adapt to the grooming process.

Grooming Basics

Before you begin grooming your pet, you'll need the following supplies:

- a brush and comb
- cotton balls
- special kitten (or cat) toothbrush and feline-safe toothpaste (do not use toothpaste made for people)
- nail clippers designed for use on cats (optional)

Brushing and Combing

Brushing and/or combing your cat's fur is beneficial to your pet. When you brush or comb the cat, you remove any loose hair and reduce the amount of fur that the cat will swallow when he bathes himself. If your cat (or kitten) swallows excessive amounts of hair, he can develop hairballs. Long-haired cats and kittens need some extra help in the grooming department. Breeds such as the Maine Coon and Persian have a lot of hair, and if left ungroomed, it can easily become tangled, matted, or knotted. If you have a long-haired breed, make sure you purchase a brush and comb set specially designed for long-haired cats or kittens.

Clipping the Nails

Some cat owners clip their cat's nails once a month as a part of their regular grooming ritual, but it's not 100 percent necessary. Clipping the nails will prevent your cat from scratching you or objects in your home (such as furniture). If you decide to clip your cat's nails, purchase a special cat nail clipper (do not use one designed for humans) and a styptic pencil (available in most grocery stores).

To clip your cat's nails, hold the cat in your lap and press on the paw until the claw comes out. Clip off the very end of the cat's claw. Be careful and avoid cutting into the quick (where the nerves and the blood vessels are). If you accidentally cut into the quick, apply the styptic pencil to stop the bleeding.

Veterinarians can show you how to clip your cat's nails.

If you're not comfortable with clipping your cat's nails yourself, ask the veterinarian or a pet groomer to do it for you. It's a good idea to start clipping the cat's nails when he or she is a kitten, because a grown cat may refuse to let you clip his nails.

Cleaning the Eyes and Ears

If your cat or kitten has been scratching his ears a lot, he may have ear mites. Check your pet's ears. If you see dark waxy stuff that looks like coffee grounds in his ears, take him to the veterinarian for an ear mite treatment. The vet will give you prescription ear drops and show you how to clean the cat's ears.

In general, a cat's ears should look clean and will only need a minimal amount of maintenance. Once a week, dip a cotton ball in baby oil and wipe out the cat's ears. Don't use a cotton swab—if the cat moves suddenly, you could damage his eardrum.

A cat's eyes don't need much grooming attention, either. If your kitten or cat has residue in the corners of his eyes, wipe it off with a cotton ball dipped in warm water.

Grooming Your Cat or Kitten

Declawing

Declawing is the permanent surgical removal of a cat's claws. It's natural for cats (and kittens) to scratch, but some cat owners decide to have the cat's claws removed as a way of correcting "bad scratching behaviors." Some veterinarians refuse to perform this inhumane surgery and recommend having a cat's nails clipped (or trimmed) instead. Declawing can cause psychological problems, such as aggression (biting or hissing), depression, or other antisocial behaviors. Declawing makes a cat defenseless, and a declawed cat should never be allowed to roam free outside.

Dental Care

Believe it or not, you should brush your cat's teeth as a part of his regular grooming routine. Over time, tartar and plaque will build up on your cat's teeth. If left unchecked, this could lead to tooth loss and gum disease.

Check your cat's ears on weekly basis.

Start brushing your cat's teeth at a young age so he gets used to the process. An adult cat that has never had his teeth brushed may resent it at first, so be patient and keep trying. If your adult cat absolutely refuses to let you brush his teeth, ask your veterinarian to do it for you. The vet may have to remove hardened tartar and built-up plaque if the cat has never had his teeth cleaned before.

Before you start brushing the cat's teeth, open the cat's mouth and look at his gums. They should be pink and appear healthy. (If they are swollen or bleeding, take the cat to the vet right away.) To brush the cat's teeth, put a little bit of cat-safe toothpaste on the toothbrush and brush one row of teeth at a time. (The cat or kitten may squirm and/or try to bite the toothbrush, but he will settle down when he realizes that the flavored toothpaste tastes good.) You only have to brush the outsides of the teeth because the cat's rough tongue

Brushing your cat's teeth will keep his breath manageable and his teeth healthy for years to come.

brushes the insides. Brush your cat's teeth daily if the cat enjoys it, but make sure to do it at least once a week, minimum. You may want to consider buying a special "dental formula" of dry cat food that will help keep the cat's teeth clean between brushings.

Bathing Your Cat or Kitten

Cats and kittens wash themselves several times a day, but there may be an occasion when your kitty has gotten into a mess and needs a soap and water bath. If your cat has something sticky or smelly in his coat or is covered in mud, then it's time for a bath. Most cats hate water and will not willingly want to take a bath, but if you have to wash your cat, here's how to make it easy.

Place a bath mat or towel in the bottom of the kitchen sink. (Don't try to wash the cat in the bathtub; you'll never be able to control him and you'll end up getting the bath.) The towel or bath mat will give the cat something to hold on to and he won't slip or feel

Grooming Your Cat or Kitten

Remember

Only use a shampoo that is specifically made for kittens or cats. Do not use dishwashing detergent, a bar of soap, ferret or dog shampoo, or shampoo designed for humans on your cat or kitten. The chemicals in these products are too harsh for your pet and could make your kitten or cat sick.

insecure in the sink. Add a few inches of lukewarm water in the sink and wet the cat lightly. Work a small amount of cat (or kitten) shampoo into the cat's fur, and then rinse with warm water. (Be careful not to get any shampoo or water into the cat's eyes, ears, or nose.) The cat will wash himself after his bath, so be sure to rinse all the shampoo out of the cat's coat. If you have a small kitten, be sure to adjust the depth of the water and the amount of shampoo according to the kitten's size.

After the cat or kitten has been rinsed clean, wrap him in a thick towel and dry him off. Don't let the wet cat go outside or near any open windows or doors until his fur is completely dry. You can try drying your cat or kitten with a hairdryer on a low setting, but most cats will be afraid of the hairdryer and will try to run away.

If you start grooming your kitten early, he will readily adjust to his grooming routine. An adult cat that is not used to being groomed may fuss and struggle with you until he adapts to the process. If you think your cat or kitten will put up a fight when it's grooming time, enlist the assistance of a friend or family member to help you hold the cat. Before you know it, your cat or kitten will become spoiled by all the extra attention he gets and look forward to being groomed.

Health Care for Your Cat or Kitten

Your cat or kitten can't tell you if he or she is feeling sick or if something is wrong. It's up to you, as a responsible pet owner, to take care of your cat's health care needs. This means learning to recognize the signs of an ill cat and getting your cat all the necessary vaccinations. The best way to keep your cat or kitten healthy throughout his or her lifetime is to make sure your pet gets annual veterinary checkups.

Finding a Vet

The veterinarian you choose will be vital in the health care of your cat or kitten. Finding a qualified vet in your area should be easy. If you've never owned a cat before, ask friends, neighbors,

Be sure to choose a veterinarian that is good with cats. Some vets specialize in only treating cats.

relatives, and co-workers who have cats who they trust with their pets. Odds are, they'll be happy to share their information with you. If you adopt a cat or kitten from a rescue organization, ask who their vet is and consider using that vet.

After you've gotten several recommendations, call each vet's office and ask the following questions about their practice:

- Are they a "cats only" vet clinic?

- What hours are they open? Is there a vet on-call in case of an after-hours emergency?

- What are the standard fees for office visits and vaccinations?

If you are satisfied with the answers, take a trip to the vet's office and check it out in person. Talk to the staff and the vet (if possible), and tell them you're looking for a vet for your cat or kitten. Evaluate the friendliness and helpfulness of the staff. You want to choose a veterinarian who takes time to talk to you and answers any questions you have about the office, their procedures, and animal care in general.

Don't Take Chances

If you think your cat or kitten is sick, trust your instincts and take him to the vet immediately. Don't wait to see if the cat gets better on his own or hope that the illness will just go away. In some cases, waiting can make a problem much worse, and delaying treatment could be fatal. When it comes to your pet's health, it's better to be safe than sorry. Don't attempt to diagnose any health issue on your own—take the cat to the vet.

Is My Cat or Kitten Sick?

Monitor your cat's or kitten's daily habits, including how much he eats and drinks, how many hours a day he sleeps, and how often he uses the litter box. Any drastic change in behavior is a signal that something is not right with your cat. By observing your cat and getting to know how he usually acts, you'll be able to tell when he is not acting "normal."

Signs of Illness

Cats are complex creatures, and they can have a variety of ailments. The following are signs of illness in a cat or kitten. If your cat is not acting normal and displays any of these symptoms, take him to the vet. After evaluating the circumstances, the vet will be able to provide a course of action. There could be many reasons why your cat or kitten is exhibiting these symptoms, and only a vet will be

In Case of Emergency

Once you've found a vet you like, make sure to keep the vet's name, address, phone number, and directions to the clinic in one place. If you or another family member have to rush the cat to the vet or make an emergency call, you'll want to have all the information easily accessible.

able to tell you for sure what is wrong with your cat. Signs of an ill cat or kitten include:

- bleeding
- blood in urine or stool
- coughing
- cries, hisses, or growls when picked up or petted
- diarrhea
- drooling
- excessive eating or drinking
- fever
- labored or rapid breathing
- lethargy
- limping
- loss of appetite or will not drink
- rapid weight loss (or rapid weight gain)
- runny nose and/or discharge from the eyes
- straining in the litter box with no results
- sudden personality change (biting, scratching, or hissing)
- third eyelid (haw) exposed for a prolonged period of time
- trouble walking or walking off balance
- unkempt fur
- vomiting

Common Feline Ailments

It's important to keep your cat or kitten healthy and happy, and the best way you can do that is to know how to recognize many common cat ailments. These maladies can range from having fleas to contracting a near-fatal illness. Let's take a look at the more common health concerns your cat or kitten could have.

Diarrhea

Diarrhea is unpleasant for any cat, but it can be life threatening to a tiny kitten. Kittens have very delicate systems, and diarrhea could lead to fatal dehydration if left untreated. Diarrhea can result from a variety of ailments, such as a stomach virus, overfeeding, or a parasitic infection. If your kitten or cat has diarrhea, take him to the vet for treatment.

Feline Immunodeficiency Virus (FIV)

This virus is commonly spread through bites, so if you have an indoor-only cat or kitten, you probably won't need to worry about your pet contracting this virus. FIV effects the immune system and makes a cat susceptible to chronic infections. A blood test can detect FIV, and if your cat tests positive, your vet can discuss treatment options with you. If you get your cat vaccinated against FIV, the cat will always test positive for the disease. This will taint future testing for FIV for the rest of the cat's life.

Feline Infectious Peritonitis (FIP)

There are two types of FIP. The "wet" form results in fluids collecting in the chest or abdomen, which makes it hard for the cat or kitten to breathe. A cat with the "dry" form will drink a lot of water because his kidneys are failing. There is no cure for FIP, and this disease mainly occurs in kittens and older cats because their immune systems aren't very strong. Some symptoms of FIP include anemia, fever, loss of appetite, swollen stomach, weight loss, and an unkempt coat.

Annual checkups are a must for cats. This way any problems that may come up will hopefully be caught early enough for proper treatment.

Feline Leukemia Virus (FeLV)

FeLV attacks a cat's or kitten's immune system and prevents the animal from fighting off diseases. FeLV is passed from cat to cat through direct contact via bodily fluids, and kittens can get FeLV if they nurse from an infected mother. This disease is very deadly to kittens, and approximately one-third of kittens who contract FeLV die from it. Symptoms of FeLV include anemia, blood in the stool, colds, diarrhea, loss of appetite, lethargy, weight loss, and excessive drinking.

If you have a cat and decide to adopt a new cat or kitten, always get the newcomer checked for FeLV before you allow him near your other cat(s). You don't want to accidentally expose a healthy cat or kitten to FeLV. If your new cat does test positive for FeLV, don't despair. Many animal rescue organizations or shelters specifically place FeLV-positive cats and kittens in other FeLV-positive cat households. These cats can live together comfortably for the rest of their lives. Although there is no cure for FeLV, a vaccination is available. Talk to your vet about this disease and be sure to have all your cats tested for it.

Feline Panleukopenia Virus (FPV) is a serious illness that kills nearly 90 percent of infected kittens under six months of age.

Feline Panleukopenia Virus (FPV)

FPV (also known as feline distemper) is a disease that preys on a cat's or kitten's nervous system, immune system, and bowels. Sadly, FPV kills approximately 90 percent of infected kittens under six months old. The good news is that you can immunize your cat or kitten against FPV. A healthy cat can contract FPV from a sick cat or from infected fleas. If you

Fleas are sometimes easier to see on cats that have light-colored coats.

handle a cat with FPV and then pet your healthy cat, you could transmit FPV to your cat. Some symptoms of FPV include lack of balance, falling, loss of appetite, and lethargy. If your cat or kitten is displaying these symptoms, take him to the vet immediately.

Fleas

Fleas are no fun for any feline, but an infestation of fleas can be deadly to a tiny kitten. Fleas suck blood, and enough of them can make a kitten anemic. In addition to draining the cat's blood, fleas can infect your cat with tapeworms.

If you think your cat has fleas, part the fur and look for bits of flea "dirt" (it looks like flecks of pepper). You may even spot a few fleas crawling or jumping around on your cat. If the cat or kitten has fleas, take him to the vet for treatment. There are many flea remedies available on the market, including flea collars, flea shampoos, flea dips, and "spot-on" treatments.

Some flea preventatives may be too strong for a small kitten, so ask your vet for a recommendation before treating the fleas yourself. Never use any flea product designed for dogs on a cat or kitten—it could be fatal.

Hairballs

Long-haired cats and kitten are more susceptible to hairballs than short-haired breeds. When cats groom themselves, they swallow their loose hair. Over time, the hair could become stuck in the cat's intestines and eventually lead to constipation. (Sometimes a kitten or cat will vomit up extra hair. This is normal.) If you think your cat is constipated, take him to the vet for a remedy. (In extreme cases the vet may have to operate to remove the blockage.)

You can reduce the chances of your cat getting hairballs by brushing and combing the cat regularly. This removes the extra hair, and the cat won't swallow it. You may want to consider buying a special "hairball prevention" formula of dry cat food if you have a long-haired cat or kitten. This food is high in fiber and will help any extra hair pass through the cat's system.

Heartworm

Heartworm is spread by the bite of an infected mosquito. Symptoms of heartworm include difficulty breathing, coughing, and vomiting. If you live in an area that has a high mosquito population, or you suspect that your cat may have heartworms, see the vet. He or she can prescribe a treatment method suitable for your kitten or cat.

Hookworms

A cat or kitten can die from an untreated infestation of hookworms. These worms attach themselves to the walls of the intestines and interfere with the animal's ability to utilize the nutrients from the food they consumed. A cat can get hookworms from an infected mother or from contact with a litter box that a hookworm-infected cat has used. Symptoms of hookworms include anemia, lethargy, and weight loss.

Rabies

Rabies is a very dangerous disease. It is caused by a virus and found in the saliva of an infected animal. Rabies is transmitted through

If you are unsure whether your kitty has fleas, your vet can show you what to look for.

bites. A rabid animal will act aggressive, have trouble swallowing, and may attack anything (or anyone) that gets too close. Symptoms can appear one week to one year after the initial contact. Have your cats and kittens vaccinated against this disease, especially if they are allowed to go outside and may come into contact with other animals.

Ringworm

Ringworm is a highly contagious fungal infection. If you handle a cat with ringworm, you can spread the infection to other pets. Signs of ringworm include a red circular pattern and hair loss. If you suspect your cat or kitten has ringworm, contact your vet. He or she may recommend an antifungal ointment as treatment. If your pet has ringworm, wash all his bedding in hot water and vacuum your home thoroughly.

Roundworms

Roundworms live in a cat's intestines. When the cat defecates, roundworm eggs pass out of the cat's system and lay dormant. If another animal comes into contact with the eggs and ingests them, he

Precaution

Always wash your hands thoroughly after handling a strange cat, a sick cat, or after emptying the litter box. You don't want to unwittingly transmit any bacteria or disease to your healthy pets.

will become infected. If a mother cat has roundworm, her kittens can be born with them. Signs of roundworms include a distended stomach or abdomen, lethargy, and weight loss. In some cases, you may be able to see the worms under the cat's tail or in his stool. If you suspect your cat has roundworm, take him to the vet immediately.

Tapeworms

Tapeworms are parasites that live in the intestines of kittens and cats. If left untreated, a tapeworm infestation can be fatal to a kitten. Tapeworms cause abdominal pain, an increased appetite, anemia, diarrhea, weight loss, and lethargy. If a cat has fleas, he may also have tapeworms. A flea-infected kitten could swallow tapeworm eggs when he grooms himself. If you see white or yellowish rice-like things under the base of your cat's tail, he has tapeworms. Take the cat to the vet and ask for a deworming treatment.

Cats that are kept indoors are less likely to contract diseases or get parasites than cats that are allowed to roam.

Ticks

Ticks are small brownish/black bloodsuckers that hide in the cat's ears and fur. If your cat isn't allowed outside, he shouldn't come into contact with ticks. If your cat does go outside, part his fur in various places and check him for ticks. If you find a tick, grasp its body with tweezers and pull it out slowly. Don't use matches, alcohol, salt, or other home remedies to try to remove the tick because you could seriously harm your pet. If your cat has a lot of ticks, or if you feel uncomfortable pulling

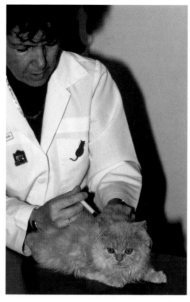

Make sure your cat receives all the necessary vaccinations he or she needs to stay healthy.

them off, take the cat to the vet and have him professionally removed.

Upper Respiratory Infections

While upper respiratory infections (or colds) are not a major concern for adult cats, they can be troublesome to a small kitten. Your kittens should be vaccinated against the most common cold viruses (feline calicivirus and feline herpesvirus) as soon as possible. An infected kitten can spread the illness to other animals in the household, so if your kitten has a cold, keep him isolated from other pets for 7 to 14 days. Symptoms of a feline cold are lack of appetite, lack of energy, sneezing, a runny nose, and watery eyes.

Urinary Tract Infection

If your cat cries out in pain when urinating, he may have a urinary tract infection. Other symptoms include bloody urine, difficulty urinating, frequent urination, or urinating outside the litter box. If your cat has these symptoms, get him to the vet immediately. If left untreated, a urinary tract infection could be fatal.

Kittens and Vaccinations

In general, kittens should receive their first series of shots at eight weeks of age. (A kitten receives immunity from diseases from his mother's milk, and is protected for the first seven or eight weeks of his life.) Your vet will schedule booster shots about three to four weeks after the initial vaccinations. After that time, your kitten should get booster shots every year (or every three years, depending on the vaccination and the vet's recommendation). Discuss the vaccination process with your vet and make sure he or she explains each vaccination in detail (what it's for) and why your kitten needs (or doesn't need) it. Ask questions if you are unsure about any aspect of your kitten's health care needs.

Vaccination Reactions

Some kittens and adult cats may have a mild reaction to a vaccination. Reaction symptoms can include fever, sneezing, loss of appetite, and lethargy. Watch your cat for a few hours after you bring him home from the vet's office, and make sure that he's acting normal. If your cat or kitten has adverse side effects such as vomiting or trouble breathing, contact the vet at once.

Giving your cat or kitten the proper care he or she needs to stay healthy is easy. The combination of a nutritious diet, regular veterinary checkups, and a safe home environment will keep your cat or kitten in good health for many years to come. Your feline friend is relying on you to take care of him for the rest of his life. Be a responsible pet owner and give your cat companion all the love and attention he needs and deserves.

Resources

ORGANIZATIONS

American Association of Cat Enthusiasts (AACE)
P.O. Box 213
Pine Brook, NJ 07058
Telephone: (973) 335-6717
E-mail: info@aaceinc.org
www.aaceinc.org

American Cat Fanciers Association (ACFA)
P.O Box 1949
Nixa, MO 65714-1949
Telephone: (417) 725-1530
E-mail: mcats@bellsouth.net
www.acfacat.com

The Cat Fanciers' Association, Inc.(CFA)
P.O. Box 1005
Manasquan, NJ 08736-0805.
Telephone: (732) 528-9797
E-mail: cfa@cfainc.org
www.cfainc.org

The International Cat Association (TICA)
P.O. Box 2684
Harlingen, TX 78551
Telephone: (956) 428-8046
E-mail: ticaeo@xanadu2.net
www.tica.org

Traditional and Classic Cat International (TCCI)
10289 Vista Point Loop
Penn Valley, CA 95946
E-mail: tccat@tccat.org
www.tccat.org

MAGAZINES

Cat Fancy
Subscription Department
P.O. Box 37196
Boone, IA 50037
Telephone: (800) 365-4421
E-mail: letters@catfancy.com
www.catfancy.com

Cats & Kittens
Pet Publishing, Inc.
7-L Dundas Circle
Greensboro, NC 27407
Telephone: (336) 292-4047
E-mail: cksubscriptions@petpublishing.com
www.catsandkittens.com

ANIMAL WELFARE GROUPS AND RESCUE ORGANIZATIONS

Alley Cat Allies
7920 Norfolk Avenue
Suite 600
Bethesda, MD 20814-2525
Telephone: (240) 482-1980
www.alleycat.org

American Humane Association (AHA)
63 Inverness Drive East
Englewood, CO 80112
Telephone: (303) 792-9900
www.americanhumane.org

American Society for the Prevention of Cruelty to Animals (ASPCA)
424 E. 92nd Street
New York, NY 10128-6804
Telephone: (212) 876-7700
www.aspca.org

Royal Society for the Prevention of Cruelty to Animals (RSPCA)
Telephone: 0870 3335 999
Fax: 0870 7530 284
www.rspca.org.uk

The Humane Society of the United States (HSUS)
2100 L Street, NW
Washington DC 20037
Telephone: (202) 452-1100
www.hsus.org

VETERINARY RESOURCES

Academy of Veterinary Homeopathy (AVH)
P.O. Box 9280
Wilmington, DE 19809
Telephone: (866) 652-1590
Fax: (866) 652-1590
E-mail: office@TheAVH.org
www.theavh.org

American Academy of Veterinary Acupuncture (AAVA)
100 Roscommon Drive, Suite 320
Middletown, CT 06457
Telephone: (860) 635-6300
E-mail: office@aava.org
www.aava.org

American Animal Hospital Association (AAHA)
P.O. Box 150899
Denver, CO 80215-0899
Telephone: (303) 986-2800
E-mail: info@aahanet.org
www.aahanet.org

American Holistic Veterinary Medical Association (AHVMA)
2218 Old Emmorton Road
Bel Air, MD 21015
Telephone: (410) 569-0795
E-mail: office@ahvma.org
www.ahvma.org

American Veterinary Medical Association (AVMA)
1931 North Meacham Road – Suite 100
Schaumburg, IL 60173
Telephone: (847) 925-8070
E-mail: avmainfo@avma.org
www.avma.org

British Veterinary Association (BVA)
7 Mansfield Street
London
W1G 9NQ
Telephone: 020 7636 6541
E-mail: bvahq@bva.co.uk
www.bva.co.uk

Index

Photo Credits:

Gillian Lisle, 30 (both), 39
Isabelle Francais, 14, 25, 32, 36, 44, 47, 49, 60
Joan Balzarini, 5, 56
John Tyson, 6, 8, 10-11, 40, 42
Karen Taylor, 20
Lara Stern, 19, 48
Linda Beatie, 52
Richard K. Blackmon, 38
Robert Pearcy, 4, 12, 27, 31
T.F.H. Archives, 23, 45, 51, 55, 57, 59, 61
Vince Serbin, 22